SHEIKH ZAYED

Frances LaBonte

To my sons James and Andrew LaBonte

A simplified form of English transliteration has been used for the Arabic words.
Map artwork: Tim Oliver
The map on page 24 is not an authority on international boundaries.

Published in 2006 by JERBOA BOOKS
PO Box No 333838, Dubai, UAE
www.jerboabooks.com
ISBN 9948-431-09-X
رقم إذن الطباعة: 710
التاريخ: 9 May 2006

Photo acknowledgements:
With thanks to the Center for Documentation and Research in Abu Dhabi
for providing the pictures on pp. 8, 14, 27. Thanks to BP Archive for providing
the pictures on pp. 6 (bottom), 7, 9, 10, 16. All other pictures kindly arranged and
supplied by Graeme Wilson of Media Prima, Dubai, enquiries@mediaprima.ae

Produced by Cambridge Publishing Management Ltd
Printed in India

Contents

Father of a Nation

Sheikh Zayed was the first president of the United Arab Emirates. He was born in the emirate of Abu Dhabi, in southern Arabia. There were many emirates or small countries in that area of Arabia and they were known as the Trucial States.

Each emirate had its own ruler, and Sheikh Zayed's family ruled Abu Dhabi.

Sometimes the people of the different emirates disagreed and fought with one another.

Sheikh Zayed, the first president of the United Arab Emirates.

Sheikh Zayed loved to be around children.

When Sheikh Zayed became ruler of Abu Dhabi in 1966, he said it would be better if the people of the emirates worked together. Sheikh Rashid bin Saeed al Maktoum, the ruler of Dubai, agreed. Together, they persuaded the rulers of the other emirates to join with them to form one country, called the United Arab Emirates.

Early Life

Above Sheikh Zayed bin Khalifa (Sheikh Zayed's grandfather) with his sons and tribesmen.
Right Palace Qasr Al Hosn, in Abu Dhabi. As a child, Sheikh Zayed lived here and in Al Ain.

Sheikh Zayed was born in 1918. He was named after his grandfather, Sheikh Zayed bin Khalifa, who ruled Abu Dhabi for 54 years.

6

When Sheikh Zayed was a boy, Abu Dhabi was a very poor country. There were no regular schools, so he had a private tutor, Syed Abdullah bin Ghanem. He did his homework at night by the light of a tiny lamp with a wick dipped in oil. The local Muallim taught him about his Muslim faith, Arabian poetry and history. By the age of ten Sheikh Zayed had memorised most of the verses of the Holy Qu'ran.

The Muslim faith was important to Sheikh Zayed. He built many mosques. Here he is studying a model for a new mosque.

© BP plc

Learning How to Rule

Sheikh Zayed bin Khalifa at his open-air majilis.

When Sheikh Zayed was about four years old, his father became ruler of Abu Dhabi. In most Arab homes there is a room or courtyard called a majilis where the men gather to discuss politics and their daily life. Sheikh Zayed's father was the ruler so people came to his majilis to talk about their problems and ask his advice. Young children were welcome at these gatherings, so Sheikh Zayed was able to listen and learn.

Sheikh Shakhbut, Sheikh Zayed's eldest brother, who ruled Abu Dhabi for 38 years.

© BP plc

In 1926 Sheikh Zayed's father, Sheikh Sultan, died suddenly. His successor ruled for only two years before Sheikh Shakhbut, Sheikh Zayed's eldest brother, was made ruler.

Child of the Desert

Sheikh Zayed grew up with the traditional Bedouin mode of transport – camels.

Even though Sheikh Zayed was from a ruling family, he led a simple life. As he grew to manhood, he travelled long distances by camel across the desert with Bedouin tribesmen. If he and his companions came across other Bedouin they would throw sand up into the air to show that they came in peace. He had a great love for the environment and respect for his people who lived in this harsh desert climate.

When Sheikh Zayed was 15, he went on his first big hunting trip with his falcons. He learned how to find the houbara bustard by looking for the bird's footmarks in the sand. Hunting with falcons became one of his favourite pastimes.

Sheikh Zayed with a falcon on a hunting trip.

The Search for Oil Begins

When Sheikh Shakhbut became ruler of Abu Dhabi, his mother, Sheikha Salamah bint Buti, made all her four sons promise to work together and not fight amongst themselves.

Before oil was discovered many people earned a living by fishing for pearls from boats like these, called dhows.

These men are test-drilling in the desert, looking for oil underground.

In 1936 Sheikh Shakhbut gave his brother Sheikh Zayed an important job to do. He asked him to take some foreign geologists on a tour around the west and southwest of the country. The geologists were hoping to find places where there was oil underground.

This was just the beginning of Sheikh Zayed's involvement with oil companies. One day, oil would make his country richer than he could ever have imagined.

Water for Life

In 1946 Sheikh Shakhbut made Sheikh Zayed the ruler's representative, or governor, in the eastern region of Abu Dhabi. Sheikh Zayed was now about 28 years old.

Sheikh Zayed thought it was important to make life better for the people he governed, so he decided to improve the Falaj al Sarooj.

Muwaiji fort in Al Ain, that Sheikh Zayed had built when he was governor of the eastern region of Abu Dhabi.

Sheikh Zayed surrounded by well-wishers. They were grateful for the work he had done to make their lives more comfortable.

This is a network of water channels that is more than 3,000 years old. Sheikh Zayed had the water channels repaired and made bigger. He also made sure that they were kept in good condition. This meant that people had more water for their crops and animals, and more water for bathing, too.

Protector of the People

Sheikh Zayed helped to protect Abu Dhabi from its enemies. In 1948 he helped to solve a dispute between Abu Dhabi and Dubai, which had led to clashes. In 1952 he became involved in a dispute about a village that had been occupied by Saudis. The village was in the Buraimi Oasis. Saudi Arabia, Oman and Abu Dhabi had fought over the oasis several times in the past.

© BP plc

Some of Sheikh Zayed's guards were loyal tribesmen like these.

Sheikh Zayed worked hard to build friendly relations with neighbouring states. Here he is inspecting a guard of honour with Sheikh Rashid bin Saeed al Maktoum of Dubai.

They held discussions to try to persuade the Saudis to leave but this didn't work. So in 1955 Sheikh Zayed and the Trucial Oman Scouts took back control of the area.

Setting up Schools

Sheikh Zayed about to board a plane. After he became ruler, Sheikh Zayed visited many countries and worked to promote peace.

In 1953 Sheikh Zayed travelled to Europe for the first time. He visited Britain and France with his brother and was very impressed by the hospitals and schools in those countries.

Sheikh Zayed was determined to set up schools and hospitals in Abu Dhabi. He and his brother Sheikh Khaled used their own money to open a school for boys, the Al Nayaniah Primary School, in 1959. The two sheikhs sent their own children to the school. Later, two schools for girls were opened. These were the Al Falahiyya and Al Butain schools.

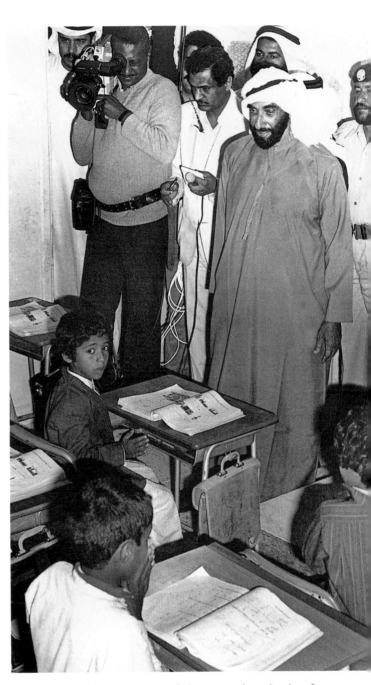

Sheikh Zayed visiting one of the many hundreds of schools he had built.

Sheikh Zayed Becomes Ruler

Bedouin with their camels in front of an oil rig. Before oil was discovered, camels were the main form of transport.

Oil was discovered in Abu Dhabi in 1958. In 1962 the first barrels of oil were sold from an oilfield off the coast at Umm Shaif. Money began to flow into the country.

Sheikh Shakhbut ruled Abu Dhabi for 38 years. For most of that time the country was poor, so he had to be careful with money.

Before the discovery of oil, Abu Dhabi's seafront looked like this. The road was just made of sand.

When money from oil sales began to make Abu Dhabi rich, he did not use the money to modernise the country in the way his people wanted him to. His family and tribal leaders decided that it would be better if he stepped down as ruler. His youngest brother, Sheikh Zayed, took over in 1966.

Forming the Federation

The British had protected Abu Dhabi and its neighbours from attack for more than a hundred years. In 1968 Britain announced that its protection would soon come to an end.

Sheikh Zayed suggested to Sheikh Rashid, the ruler of Dubai, that they should set up a federation with their neighbours.

Sheikh Zayed and other rulers, signing the agreement to set up the federation of the United Arab Emirates.

Sheikh Zayed at a meeting of the Supreme Council.

After long discussions, the emirates of Abu Dhabi, Dubai, Sharjah, Umm al Qaiwain, Ajman and Fujairah signed an agreement to set up the federation on 2 December 1971. Ras al Khaimah joined in February 1972.

The federation of emirates is called the United Arab Emirates (UAE). The government of the UAE makes decisions about relationships with other countries, but local rulers make decisions that affect only their areas of the country.

A Modern Country

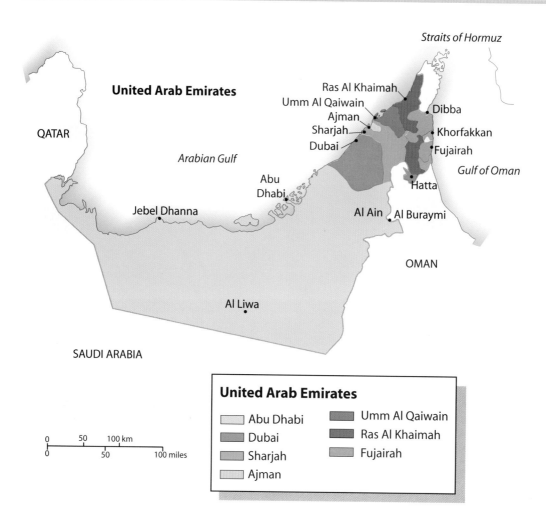

A map showing the different emirates that make up the UAE.

Sheikh Zayed became the first president of the United Arab Emirates. The rulers of the emirates vote every five years to choose a new president and they decided to re-elect Sheikh Zayed five times.

Since the UAE was set up, over 500 government schools have been built, so UAE parents don't have to pay for their children to go to school. There are colleges of higher education and a university at Al Ain. Health care is available to all.

In the early 1970s there were only about 60,000 houses in the emirates but now there are over 500,000 homes. The government has built 100,000 houses to help people who cannot afford to pay for homes themselves.

Modern Abu Dhabi, with its high-rise buildings and busy highways.

Keeping Traditions Alive

Sheikh Zayed did not want people to forget the old ways. Sometimes he went on traditional hunting trips where he slept in a simple tent.

Sheikh Zayed thought it was important to modernise the emirates, but he did not want people to forget their old way of life. He said, 'A nation without a past has no present or future.' Sheikh Zayed also wanted to look after Abu Dhabi's wildlife and the natural environment.

The old palace of Qasr Al Hosn sits among the modern buildings of Abu Dhabi.

Heritage villages have been set up where people can see traditional Bedouin tents, palm houses and souks. Sheikh Zayed's wife, Sheikha Fatima, has been involved in making sure that traditional crafts are passed on to young people and has paid great attention to women's welfare.

Sheikh Zayed visiting a handicraft exhibition.

A Lasting Legacy

A picture of Sheikh Zayed on a building.

Sheikh Zayed's long life came to an end on 2 November 2004.
His dream of creating a modern, peaceful country that kept its
traditions had come true. He was a deeply religious man who
was against terrorism. He thought about the future of his
country, provided education and health care for his people and
supported women's rights. He was generous with his wealth,
which he shared with people in need in more than forty other
countries throughout the world.

Sheikh Zayed with Sheikh Khalifa, his eldest son and successor.

Sheikh Zayed with all his sons.

Like all good leaders, he trained someone to take over from him when he died. His eldest son, Sheikh Khalifa, was elected the new president of the UAE when his father died. He will carry on his father's work. In nearly four decades Sheikh Zayed wisely guided the country from tents and camels to modern homes, computers and cars. He was truly the Father of the Nation.

Time Line

1918	Sheikh Zayed is born in Al Ain. The exact date of his birth is not known because no written records were kept at that time.
1926	Sheikh Sultan, his father, dies.
1928	Sheikh Zayed's eldest brother, Sheikh Shakhbut, becomes ruler of Abu Dhabi.
1931	Sheikh Zayed goes on his first big trip hunting for houbara with his falcons.
1936–1937	Takes geologists from an oil company to explore parts of west and southwest Abu Dhabi.
1946	Becomes the ruler's representative in Abu Dhabi's eastern region.
1950s	Mends and improves an ancient water system to improve agriculture.
1953	Makes his first trip to Europe.
1955	Settles Buraimi Oasis dispute.
1959	First primary school funded with his own money is set up.
1962	Abu Dhabi earns money from oil for the first time.
1966	Sheikh Zayed is chosen as ruler of Abu Dhabi to replace his brother.

Sheikh Zayed at prayer.

UAE soldiers handing out food supplies to help starving people in Somalia.

1968	British forces begin to leave the Arabian Gulf area.
1971	Federation of United Arab Emirates (UAE) is formed.
	The UAE joins the Arab League and the United Nations.
1974	Sheikh Zayed sets aside 28% of Abu Dhabi's income for the assistance of Arab, Islamic and developing countries.
1977	Establishment of the UAE's first university at Al Ain.
1981	Sheikh Zayed helps form the Arabian Gulf Cooperation Council (GCC).
1990	Condemns the Iraqi invasion of Kuwait.
1991	Orders the setting up of a marriage fund to help young people in the UAE to pay for their weddings.
1993	Condemns the use of violence in the name of religion.
1997	Calls on women to join the Federal National Council.
2001	Receives a World Food Day medal from the United Nations Food and Agriculture Organization in recognition of his efforts to help the poor of the world.
2002	Rejects links with terrorism and asks the leaders of Iraq to step down and go into exile to avoid war.
2004	Sheikh Zayed dies.

Index